DISCARD

DETROIT PUBLIC LIBRARY

CHILDREN'S LIBRARY
5201 WOODWARD AVE.
DETROIT, MI 48202-4093

DATE DUE

BC-3

11/00 CL

BASKETBALL LEGENDS

Kareem Abdul-Jabbar
Charles Barkley
Larry Bird
Kobe Bryant
Wilt Chamberlain
Clyde Drexler
Julius Erving
Patrick Ewing
Kevin Garnett
Anfernee Hardaway
Tim Hardaway
The Head Coaches
Grant Hill
Juwan Howard
Allen Iverson
Magic Johnson
Michael Jordan
Shawn Kemp
Jason Kidd
Reggie Miller
Alonzo Mourning
Hakeem Olajuwon
Shaquille O'Neal
Gary Payton
Scottie Pippen
David Robinson
Dennis Rodman
John Stockton
Keith Van Horn
Antoine Walker
Chris Webber

CHELSEA HOUSE PUBLISHERS

BASKETBALL LEGENDS

TIM HARDAWAY

Dan Hirshberg

*Introduction by
Chuck Daly*

CHELSEA HOUSE PUBLISHERS
Philadelphia

Produced by Combined Publishing, Inc.

CHELSEA HOUSE PUBLISHERS

Editor in Chief: Stephen Reginald
Managing Editor: James Gallagher
Production Manager: Pamela Loos
Art Director: Sara Davis
Director of Photography: Judy L. Hasday
Senior Production Editor: Lisa Chippendale
Publishing Coordinator: James McAvoy
Cover Design and Digital Illustration: Keith Trego

Cover Photos: AP/Wide World Photos

Copyright © 1999 by Chelsea House Publishers, a division of Main Line Book Co. All rights reserved. Printed and bound in the United States of America.

The Chelsea House World Wide Web site address is
http://www.chelseahouse.com

First Printing

1 3 5 7 9 8 6 4 2

Library of Congress Cataloging-in-Publication Data

Hirshberg, Dan.
  Tim Hardaway / Daniel Hirshberg.
    p.   cm. — (Basketball legends)
  Includes bibliographical references (p.   ) and index.
  Summary: A biography of the high scoring point guard who began NBA career with the Golden State Warriors and was traded to the Miami Heat in 1996.
  ISBN 0-7910-5007-6 (hc)
  1. Hardaway, Tim, 1966–   —Juvenile literature. 2. Basketball players—United States—Biography—Juvenile literature.
[1. Hardaway, Tim, 1966–   . 2. Basketball players. 3. Afro-Americans—Biography.] I. Title. II. Series.
GV884.H243H57   1998
796.323'092—dc21
[b]   98-45045
                                                    CIP
                                                    AC

CONTENTS

BECOMING A
BASKETBALL LEGEND   6
CHUCK DALY

CHAPTER 1
MIAMI'S LITTLE BIG MAN   9

CHAPTER 2
PLAYING ON A REAL TEAM   17

CHAPTER 3
DEEP IN THE HEART OF TEXAS   25

CHAPTER 4
A DRAFT DAY SURPRISE   35

CHAPTER 5
A NEW BEGINNING IN MIAMI   47

CHAPTER 6
THE ELUSIVE RING   57

CHRONOLOGY   61
STATISTICS   62
FURTHER READING   63
INDEX   64

BECOMING A BASKETBALL LEGEND

Chuck Daly

What does it take to be a basketball superstar? Two of the three things it takes are easy to spot. Any great athlete must have excellent skills and tremendous dedication. The third quality needed is much harder to define, or even put in words. Others call it leadership or desire to win, but I'm not sure that explains it fully. This third quality relates to the athlete's thinking process, a certain mentality and work ethic. One can coach athletic skills, and while few superstars need outside influence to help keep them dedicated, it is possible for a coach to offer some well-timed words in order to keep that athlete fully motivated. But a coach can do no more than appeal to a player's will to win; how much that player is then capable of ensuring victory is up to his own internal workings.

In recent times, we have been fortunate to have seen some of the best to play the game. Larry Bird, Magic Johnson, and Michael Jordan had all three components of superstardom in full measure. They brought their teams to numerous championships, and made the players around them better. (They also made their coaches look smart.)

I myself coached a player who belongs in that class, Isiah Thomas, who helped lead the Detroit Pistons to consecutive NBA crowns. Isiah is not tall—he's just over six feet—but he could do whatever he wanted with the ball. And what he wanted to do most was lead and win.

All the players I mentioned above and those whom this series will chronicle are tremendously gifted athletes, but for the most part, you can't play professional basketball at all unless you have excellent skills. And few players get to stay on their team unless they are willing to dedicate themselves to improving their talents even more, learning about their opponents, and finding a way to join with their teammates and win.

It's that third element that separates the good player from the superstar, the memorable players from the legends of the game. Superstars know when to take over the game. If the situation calls for a defensive stop, the superstars stand up and do it. If the situation calls for a key pass, they make it. And if the situation calls for a big shot, they want the ball. They don't want the ball simply because of their own glory or ego. Instead they know—and their teammates know—that they are the ones who can deliver, regardless of the pressure.

The words "legend" and "superstar" are often tossed around without real meaning. Taking a hard look at some of those who truly can be classified as "legends" can provide insight into the things that brought them to that level. All of them developed their legacy over numerous seasons of play, even if certain games will always stand out in the memories of those who saw them. Those games typically featured amazing feats of all-around play. No matter how great the fans thought the superstars were, these players were capable of surprising the fans, their opponents, and occasionally even themselves. The desire to win took over, and with their dedication and athletic skills already in place, they were capable of the most astonishing achievements.

CHUCK DALY, now the head coach of the Orlando Magic, guided the Detroit Pistons to two straight NBA championships, in 1989 and 1990. He earned a gold medal as coach of the 1992 U.S. Olympic basketball team—the so-called "Dream Team"—and was inducted into the Pro Basketball Hall of Fame in 1994.

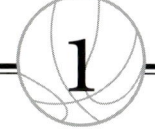

MIAMI'S LITTLE BIG MAN

The Miami Heat battled back after nearly losing the Eastern Conference semifinal series to the New York Knicks. But now, in the third quarter of the seventh and deciding game, they were without their foul-plagued center, Alonzo Mourning. Miami was in trouble, its once huge 17-point lead dwindling.

Could the Heat's 1996-97 Atlantic Division winning season be coming to an abrupt end?

The Heat needed help, and it came from an unlikely source. The team's smallest player, 6-foot point guard Tim Hardaway, stepped in during the team's time of need and became their biggest asset. It was nothing new for Hardaway. The Chicago native has been playing big ever since he started for his school's eighth grade basketball team—as a sixth grader.

With time closing in on the Heat in front of their hometown crowd, Hardaway needed to play

The Miami Heat's Tim Hardaway raises his arms in celebration at the end of an NBA Eastern Conference semifinal game against the New York Knicks.

Tim Hardaway

Dan Majerle hugs his Miami Heat teammate Tim Hardaway after he sank a crucial three-pointer against the Orlando Magic in the Eastern Conference playoffs on May 4, 1997.

big again if his team was going to go on and face the Chicago Bulls in the Eastern Conference finals.

Hardaway had played well during the regular season and in the opening playoff series against the Orlando Magic. The Heat toppled their Florida neighbors in five games, but it wasn't easy. In the end, it had come down to Hardaway.

The Magic had come back from a 2-0 deficit in the first round playoff series to win Game 3, even though they trailed by 20 at one point. Orlando then won Game 4 to force the fifth showdown on the court.

In the final game, Miami blew a 16-point lead with nine minutes to go, allowing the Magic to draw to within four points, 82-78, with three minutes left. Hardaway was told by his coach, Pat Riley, to take control of the game.

Hardaway responded, and the Magic didn't have a chance. With home team Miami holding onto an 84-80 lead with 43.3 seconds to go, Hardaway fired in a 20-foot jump shot for a six-point lead. After Orlando's Anfernee Hardaway countered with a three-point bomb, Tim Hardaway dribbled toward the three-point line and pulled up close to the arc. He shot with 14.1 seconds left, and the ball sailed through the net. The basket gave Miami an 89-83 lead.

Soon, the game was history, with the Heat winning, 91-83.

"I made two tough shots that needed to be made," Tim Hardaway said. "It was a good feeling."

Anfernee Hardaway, who is no relation to Tim, had 33 points, 10 rebounds, and six assists in the fifth game. He noted the obvious: "As great a player as Tim is, you can't hold him down for

MIAMI'S LITTLE BIG MAN

The New York Knicks' Patrick Ewing and Charlie Ward guard Tim Hardaway as he drives to the basket.

an entire series. When they needed him the most, he took it upon himself [to win the game]."

New York, who had swept Charlotte three straight in their opening playoff series, took a quick one-game lead in the opener in Miami, 88-79, despite 21 points from Hardaway. Hardaway kept it up in the second game, leading the Heat to an 88-84 victory. The All-Star finished with 34 points, eight rebounds, and four assists, but it was a sensational second quarter blitz that had everyone shaking their heads.

In the last three minutes of the second quarter, Hardaway fired in 13 consecutive points. Starting with a 25-footer, Hardaway went on to score with a drive along the baseline, with a soft underhand layup, and with a three-pointer. Then, as the buzzer sounded to end the period, he drilled home a 28-footer that sent the Miami crowd into a frenzy. As Hardaway headed for the dressing room, the scoreboard lit up his 25-point effort in the first half.

"He just took over," Riley said afterwards. "He's capable of doing that. Tonight his shot was dropping."

With 50 seconds left in the fourth quarter and the Knicks still in range, Hardaway put away New York for good when he hit a driving basket in the lane over the outstretched arms of 7-foot All-Star center Patrick Ewing. "I went to the hole and made something happen," Hardaway told reporters. "It was a tough shot over Patrick Ewing."

The Knicks won Game 3, 77-73, and Game 4, 89-76, bringing the series to 3-1. It didn't look good for the Heat, a team that had won its first playoff game in history a couple of weeks earlier. The odds seemed to be against them. Only five other teams had been able to come back in the NBA playoffs from a 3-1 deficit to win a series. Another bad omen—they had now lost six of seven games to the Knicks.

But the Miami players were determined to win, especially Hardaway, who was the Heat's leader in points, assists, steals, and minutes played during the regular season. Although Hardaway had a disappointing effort with only 16 points in Game 5, Miami won, 96-81. Game 5, however, will forever be remembered for a fight that broke out late in the game, rather than any on-court highlights.

The play had been physical throughout the series, beginning with Game 1, when Heat reserve Isaac Austin hit New York's Ward in the head with his forearm after one time-out. In the third quarter of Game 2, Miami's P. J. Brown and New York's Charles Oakley were whistled for technicals for grappling with each other. And in Game 4, Oakley was given a technical foul for kneeing a Heat player during one rough play.

The physical nature of the series was no surprise. Everyone—the players, the coaches, the media, the fans—expected it, because that was the way it had been all season long whenever Miami and New York met. With the playoffs, the feelings only intensified. The Atlantic Division rivals each felt they had something to prove. The second-place Knicks wanted to show up their former coach, Riley. And Miami was out to prove that its first-place finish was no fluke. Both teams expected a physical series—and they got it.

The series erupted into a full-fledged war in Miami late in the fifth game. With 1:55 left, the Knicks' Oakley was ejected for shoving Mourning too hard. Two seconds later, after Hardaway gave the Heat a comfortable lead by making two free throws, Brown of the Heat and Charlie Ward of the Knicks ended up in the middle of a melee.

As Hardaway took his second shot, Brown and Ward began to mix it up as they waited for the ball to drop into the net. Suddenly, Brown picked up Ward and tossed him to the ground. John Wallace of New York then jumped on Brown. The rest of the players on the court piled onto each

Tim Hardaway attempts to shoot around the defense of New York Knick Buck Williams.

other and a few Knicks came off the bench to join in.

When the dust had cleared, Brown and Ward were thrown out of the game, and the next day, the NBA suspended Brown for two games and Ward for one. In addition, the Knicks lost Ewing and guard Allan Houston for a game because they came off the bench during a fight, a practice strictly forbidden by the NBA. John Starks of New York was also ejected from the game and suspended for Game 7 for making an obscene gesture toward a fan. For the last game of the series, the Knicks would also be without Larry Johnson, who was suspended for coming off the bench.

With Game 6, Hardaway brought the focus back to basketball, taking control and playing big with 20 points, eight assists, and six rebounds. His three-pointer late in the fourth quarter tied the game for Miami, setting the stage for a stretch run that eventually pushed depressed New York fans to head for the exits. Miami posted a 95-90 victory, and, incredibly, had tied the series 3-3 to force a Game 7 in Miami.

Reeling from two straight losses to the Heat, the undermanned Knicks quickly fell behind in Game 7. New York was down by 17 at the half, 49-32, in part because of an 18-0 first quarter run by Miami. The Knicks finally got it together, but not until the second half.

The Knicks' hopes rose a bit in the third period, but not for long. Near the end of the third quarter, Hardaway swiped at the Knicks' collective egos with a barrage of three-pointers. The shots drained through the basket one after another, some hitting the backboard first, some touching the rim, some swishing the net. In one span of 90 seconds, he sank three of them.

While Mourning sat and watched, Hardaway slashed the Knicks for 18 of his team's 22 third-quarter points—16 points alone came during a five-minute burst of play. He made six of 10 three-pointers in the game, four of seven in just the third quarter. Overall, he made seven of 10 shots in that dazzling third quarter. When it was over, the Heat had a dominating 71-54 lead, courtesy of Hardaway's personal assault.

"The third quarter was trouble," Hardaway said after the game. "The big fella [Mourning] was in [foul] trouble, and we couldn't get the offense going. I just knew I had to break out. So I just started making shots, 3 after 3 after 3."

It happened so fast that his father, Donald, missed it all. He told a reporter later that he was looking to buy ice cream for Timothy Hardaway Jr. By the time he got back to his seat, his son had jolted the Knicks right out of the game. Twelve minutes later it was official: Miami 101, New York 90.

"I'd never had a quarter like that before," said Hardaway. "It [the outcome] might have been different if I hadn't."

It was some quarter—and some game. When the final buzzer finally sounded and fans heard Frank Sinatra singing "Chicago" over the sound system, the stat sheet showed Hardaway with a team playoff record of 38 points and seven assists.

The New York Knicks, like the Orlando Magic before them, learned a lesson. They discovered that Tim Hardaway, diminutive compared to his colleagues in the NBA, plays like the biggest man on the court.

2
PLAYING ON A REAL TEAM

Born September 1, 1966, in Chicago, Tim Hardaway developed a love for basketball by the time he could crawl. He can thank his father for that. Donald Hardaway gave Tim his first basketball while he was still in the crib. From the time he could walk, Tim Hardaway liked playing with a basketball. Dribbling and passing to anyone within throwing distance, he learned to shoot underhand at first and then overhand as he got older. His mother, Gwendolyn, supported and nurtured his love of the game.

As a toddler, he might not have understood the game, but he sensed the excitement. There were many nights when Tim would go to the playgrounds where his father Donald was—and still is—considered a legend. Indeed, on the Chicago playground circuit, 6'5" Donald Hardaway was considered one of the best. He played in two or three leagues a week, banging away with guys his age, and as he got older, against

As a youth, Tim Hardaway learned how to play basketball on the playgrounds of Chicago. Here he drives to the hoop in the NBA.

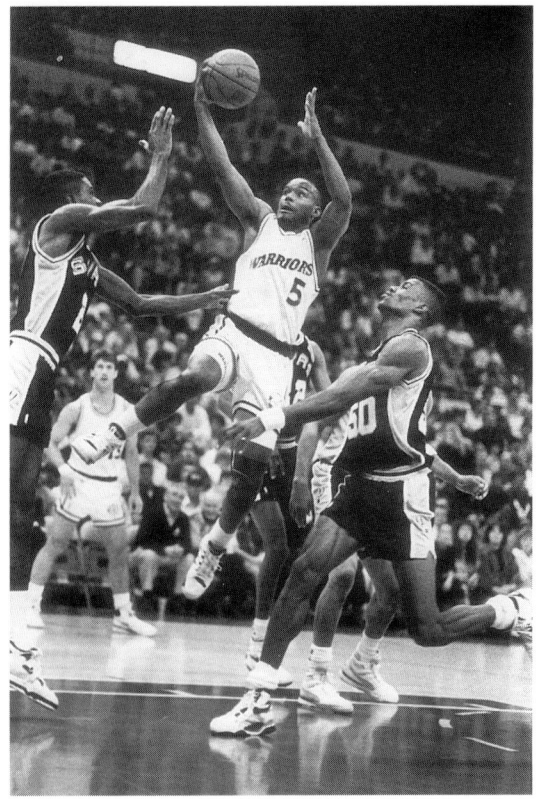

With the help of his father and high school coach, Hardaway learned to play tough and smart.

guys half his age. It didn't matter. Tim's father played them all.

An excellent athlete, Donald showed considerable promise on the court while growing up in Chicago. But after his sophomore year in high school, he decided to quit school and enlist in the Army. He returned to Chicago three years later, and it was as if he never missed a beat—he would dazzle the playground crowds night after night. He dazzled them until he was 37 and bad knees finally did him in.

When he couldn't play anymore, Donald turned his attention to Tim, whom he taught the intricacies of basketball, helping to develop the skills that would someday take his son to the NBA. Like his father, Tim dazzled kids his own age, as well as some who were much older, at the playgrounds. He quickly learned that just because someone might be physically tougher than you on the court, it doesn't mean they can outplay you.

"On the playgrounds, you got to outsmart people who play tough," he told a reporter years later while in college. On the playgrounds "I learned to create things. You get into certain situations and you revert back to what you did on the playgrounds [and do what's necessary to make a play happen]."

Although he loved hooping it up on the playgrounds, Tim was chomping at the bit from an early age to play on a real team. At Kohn Elementary School, he couldn't wait for the day when he could play on the sixth-grade team. Donald Pittman, the school's coach, remembers an enthusiastic youngster who did whatever he could to get the coach's attention.

"You could tell that Tim loved basketball," said Pittman. "He got started with me by hanging around the gym a lot. He wanted to play early. I told him he was too young, but that I'd let him be my ball boy and do some things to help the team."

By the time he was in fifth grade, Hardaway was ready to play on the sixth-grade team. Instantly, he took charge.

"He was a fifth grader playing on the sixth-grade team, and he was just so far superior than the kids on that team it was obvious this guy was something special," said Pittman. "He was like a natural point guard. He was able to run the team and he could score."

In sixth grade, Hardaway became the starting point guard on Pittman's eighth-grade team. In a league that featured some very good schools, Hardaway had three outstanding seasons. More often that not, he single-handedly won games for Kohn.

"We had a 50-point club in the school," Pittman said. "Over this period of time Tim probably had no less than 40 games where he scored 50 points or more in a game. That's how good he was. And remember, this league I'm talking about had no slouches. There were some guys who went through this league who became stars [in high school, college, and in the NBA]."

Around this time, Hardaway had to deal with family problems as his parents went through a divorce. It didn't seem to affect his play on the court. He quickly proved that not only could he score, he could also do the other things that make for a well-rounded player. Everyone he played with, including the older guys, looked up to Hardaway as the team leader. And just as he would do years later in high school, college, and in the NBA, Hardaway made the people around him better players—and better coaches.

"At a young age he was able to run a team, but what really stood out in my mind is how easy he made things for me as a coach," said Pittman. "He actually had me thinking that I was this great coach . . . Tim had been my point guard on the eighth-grade team for so many years, and I just didn't realize how good he was until he left. Now I had to go back to structuring plays, and these plays that we were running so well with Tim, all of a sudden they weren't the same anymore."

During his eighth-grade season, several Chicago high school coaches took notice. Bob Walters at Carver High School was one of them. Carver High School had historically enjoyed some fine seasons. It had graduated two other professional basketball players—Terry Cummings in the NBA and women's basketball star Yolanda Griffith. Another graduate was former New York Knick Cazzie Russell, who had led Carver to its last city championship game in the 1960s.

Carver had once ruled the Chicago basketball scene and was now attempting to regain its foothold. Walters saw Hardaway as the kind of kid who could help lead Carver to the top. With the blessing of his parents—and with Pittman coming on board as an assistant coach—Tim enrolled at Carver in the fall of 1981.

In September that year, a confident Hardaway stepped into Carver High School. While there were some rumors that Hardaway went to Carver because of a promise to start in his freshman year, they were just that—rumors. But rumors or not, it didn't take long for Hardaway to move into the starting point-guard position at Carver after beginning the season on the junior varsity team.

"The season started in November and by the end of the next month, December, he moved up to varsity," said Pittman.

Soon enough, a senior was benched and Hardaway got the starting nod. Although there was resentment from some of the older athletes, Hardaway quickly proved the move was a smart one—even if he was just a ninth grader.

"Anytime a freshman comes in [and starts] there is going to be some resentment," said Dan Finn, a teacher at Carver. "It probably made for healthy competition. You kind of felt bad for the seniors, but then Tim was a good ballplayer, too. He could penetrate, he developed the crossover dribble. He could really light it up."

During his four seasons at Carver, Hardaway found ways to score, even if he wasn't the smoothest shooter around. "He had an uncanny ability to get to the basket," said Pittman. "He could do it so well. At that particular time there was no three-point play unless you went to the basket and got fouled. Going to the basket was the thing to do. The jump shot wasn't as big a need. Yet he always had the ability to score, inside and outside."

In high school, Hardaway began to develop his now patented crossover dribble, in which he dribbles the ball side to side and then makes a move past his outwitted opponent. His ability to slip past opponents earned him the nickname "Tim Bug."

The high school standout looked to another Chicago native for inspiration—NBA star Isiah

Tim Hardaway developed a now patented crossover dribble while still in high school. Here he dribbles the ball as a Warrior in the NBA.

Thomas of the Detroit Pistons. "Isiah was my idol when I was growing up," Hardaway said. "He played the game to have fun with it and was flashy and all that stuff. I have fun when I play the game, too. Lots of fun."

With Thomas serving as his inspiration, Hardaway lit up the court for four seasons, culminating in a sensational senior year. With its spunky point guard leading the way, Carver made it to the city championship game. But Carver was defeated by San Simeon High School, a powerhouse led by Hardaway's childhood buddy, Nick Anderson, who now plays for the Orlando Magic. San Simeon had figured out how the Carver team operated, having lost to it twice before.

The loss, although tough to take at the time, could not dampen an otherwise superb campaign by the senior Hardaway and his team under the coaching of Walters.

"Coach Walters was a no-nonsense type guy, a bottom line guy," said Pittman, adding that Walters also coached football. "He had the foresight to understand that Timmy was his future if he wanted to be a successful coach. He basically turned the team over to Tim for the four years that he was there. And he was rewarded by going to the city championship game."

The championship game in 1985 was a splendid memory for Carver, Hardaway, his teammates, and Walters. Two years later, without much warning, Walters was dead from cancer.

Over the years, Hardaway has remembered his coach in many ways, donating money to the American Cancer Society for every assist he made in certain seasons. He also sent children with cancer to Sea World for a day of fun and donated money to The Children's Caring Cancer Center.

To say there were dozens of scouts hounding Hardaway at every corner would be untrue. In fact, very few scouts gave Hardaway much of a serious look. There were several likely reasons.

Although he was a terrific point guard, Hardaway wasn't very tall. And Carver, although it made it to the city championship, still was not considered one of Chicago's elite basketball schools and didn't attract as many scouts as some of the other area schools. Walters, being a relatively new coach, didn't have the connections a veteran coach might have had.

Finally, some said Hardaway wasn't good enough for college ball because he did not have a picture-perfect shot, with a few folks referring to his shot as a knuckleball. The result? Hardaway wasn't really recruited at all.

It wasn't until a tenacious assistant coach from the University of Texas talked one of college's legendary coaches into giving Hardaway a look that he finally got a chance to prove himself on the collegiate level.

3
DEEP IN THE HEART OF TEXAS

Only two colleges showed any interest in Tim Hardaway. They were Western Illinois and the University of Texas at El Paso (UTEP). And while Western Illinois pursued Hardaway, UTEP easily won the battle, even though it took a lot of persistence by an assistant coach named Russ Bradburd. A native of Chicago, Bradburd believed in Hardaway from the beginning, but he had to make UTEP's coach, Don Haskins, a believer, too.

"Russ just begged me, just begged me to get Hardaway," said Haskins, who has been the Miners' head coach since 1961. "I kept saying to him that we didn't need another guy who couldn't shoot. But he was persistent. Russ gets full credit for realizing that this guy was going to be a player. He would not have been at UTEP if it wasn't for him."

Bradburd, now an assistant at New Mexico State, was in his first year at UTEP when he came

Reaching for the ball and an NBA career, Tim Hardaway played his heart out for his college team.

upon Hardaway during a visit to the Chicago area.

"We were looking for a point guard and whenever I'd talk to somebody, the coaches or whoever up there, they would say that there's this one kid whose as good as any of them," said Bradburd. "This kid Hardaway from Carver. But he wasn't on any of my scouting reports."

Bradburd finally got to see Hardaway in action, not in a high school game, but in a playground game at South Shore Park, a few short blocks from Hardaway's home. It was a windy day in the Windy City, the kind of day when shots usually miss their mark because of the conditions. With the wind blowing, it seemed unlikely Hardaway's corkscrew shot would ever see net.

"The first time I saw him play it was windy as heck, yet he made every shot," said Bradburd. "I thought, 'this is weird. Here's this kid who they say can't shoot, and here he is in the wind making all these shots.'"

Bradburd reported back to Haskins, who was skeptical. After much nudging, however, Haskins relented and agreed to see Hardaway for himself. And so, Haskins, along with another assistant coach, Tim Floyd, ventured to Chicago to see Hardaway. This time, Hardaway was playing in a pick-up game at the high school. The point guard was on that day, showing great court awareness, throwing perfect alley-oop passes to teammates for easy baskets, and showing off some superb moves to the hoop. The coach was sold.

"I really liked what I saw," said Haskins. "He still couldn't shoot, but I liked his work ethic and enthusiasm."

In the fall of 1985, Hardaway began his collegiate career at UTEP. El Paso is located on the western edge of Texas, minutes from Mexico to the south and New Mexico to the north. It is light years away from Chicago, in distance and in lifestyle, but Hardaway was looking forward to a new challenge under a new coach.

Haskins was a legend by the time Hardaway entered UTEP. The coach, who had amassed 704 career wins through the 1997-98 season, making him one of the winningest college coaches ever, had played college ball himself under another legendary coach, Henry Iba at Oklahoma State. Over the years, Haskins, a member of the Basketball Hall of Fame, had won a national championship, seven Western Athletic Conference (WAC) crowns, and made the NCAA tournament fourteen times. In 1966, his NCAA championship–winning team upset Kentucky, 72-65, at Cole Fieldhouse in College Park, Maryland.

Hardaway, playing behind point guard Jeep Jackson, started just a handful of games in his first year, finishing with 4.1 points per game and ranking fourth on the team in assists. It was a great year for UTEP, which racked up a 27-6 mark. The Miners were led by Dave Feitl and Juden Smith, who had 16.6 and 13.7 points per game. UTEP won the WAC regular season title and the postseason tournament before falling in the first round of the NCAA tournament to Bradley, 83-65.

For Hardaway, UTEP was a bit of a shock that first year. He was used to playing a run-and-gun style at Carver. At UTEP, it was more of a half-court game that featured a slower pace. Rather than get frustrated, Hardaway was determined

Tim Hardaway flies through the air while playing college basketball for the University of Texas at El Paso.

to learn the new system and become a better player.

"In high school he would fire up outlet passes, but with Haskins, it was a slower style," said Bradburd. "All of a sudden, we weren't really a good place for Tim to showcase his strengths because we were more of a half-court game, not a run-and-gun style by any means. What Tim really excelled in was in a run-and-gun game. But what it made him do, it forced him to play another style and do some things he wasn't that good at. In a half-court game you're not going to get a lot of layups off the fast break which is what Tim did in high school and later in the pros with Golden State. When it's a half-court game, you have to shoot from the perimeter.

"All of a sudden, in order to play more, Tim had to get his game under control. He had to learn to make decisions in the half court. He learned how to become successful in a half-court game. In that regard, UTEP became the perfect place for Tim. As it turned out, he played well for us, got a lot of assists and all. But we never really got to see what Tim could really do because of the system. In actuality, Tim sacrificed his game for our game."

Hardaway took over the starting point guard role for the 1987-88 season and again the Miners had a fine season, with Hardaway averaging 10 points and 4.8 assists a contest. UTEP went

25-7 as Jackson, Chris Sandle, and Mike Richmond all averaged more than 12 points per game. The Miners won the WAC regular season crown, lost in the WAC playoffs, and entered the NCAA tournament, knocking off Arizona in the first round but getting nipped by Iowa, 84-82, in the second. Hardaway punched in 11 points in the loss to Iowa.

By his junior year, Hardaway was ready to take his game to another level. If you ask Haskins, though, he takes little credit for Hardaway's improvement as a ballplayer.

"It wouldn't have made any difference where Tim had gone, he was going to become a great player because he was bound and determined to become one," said Haskins. "It was not because of me that he got better. He did it through dedication. He was as dedicated to practice as anyone I've ever had here. I'm sitting here right now and it's 10 in the morning and if Hardaway was here and he wasn't in class, well then he'd be down in the gym shooting. He is really a self-made player. A lot of it came in the off-season. When Tim came back after his freshman year he was a much better player because he'd work hard in the summer. After his sophomore year he comes back, and now I'm looking at a junior who has improved immensely. He'd play against good competition in Chicago. It was the same thing after his junior year.

"Tim was relentless with his work ethic. When he was a freshman, Jeep Jackson fouled out against Wyoming and they went after Tim. They kept fouling him, forcing him to the line. Tim didn't make many and we lost the game. But that was the end of that. The next year he could make free throws. That's the way he was. He took care of those things. So after thousands and thousands of hours of practice, he's now a great player in the NBA."

Hardaway, who studied criminal justice at UTEP, still didn't have a smooth shot when he started his junior year, but he was one of the team's key players. Although the team stumbled a bit, finishing 23-10, winning no titles, and getting bounced from the NCAA tournament in the first round, Hardaway moved into the team leader role. If the team was getting out of control on the court, it was Hardaway who brought calm. Hardaway's numbers got better, too, despite an ankle injury late in the season. He was now averaging 13.6 points, 5.7 assists (a school record 183 for the year), and nearly three rebounds a game. His fast hands also made him a team leader in steals. At season's end, he was named to the All-WAC team.

During the WAC postseason tournament in 1988, Hardaway really turned some heads. With UTEP down to just eight players because of injuries, Hardaway was the glue that held the Miners together to win two games before losing in the final to Wyoming by four points. In that contest, Hardaway finished with 21 points, nine assists, six rebounds, and five steals.

"Nobody gave us a chance to win any games [in the WAC tournament]," said Haskins, who admitted he felt that way too because of the status of his injury-depleted team. "But Tim showed an incredible amount of poise."

In his senior year, Hardaway became the toast of El Paso. He led the team in points (22 per game), assists (5.4), and steals, and averaged four rebounds per game. In one December game,

Hardaway signs autographs for some young basketball fans.

he had 30 points against Indiana and went over the 1,000 point mark in his career.

By then, El Paso wasn't the only place interested in Hardaway. The rest of the country was paying attention. Hardaway was widely regarded as one of the best point guards in the west, if not the best. "Down in El Paso there's a kid by the name of Tim Hardaway," said basketball analyst Dick Vitale during one of his broadcasts. "He's a senior out of Chicago, and he is one tenacious competitor. He is the most underrated point guard in college basketball."

Bill Musselman, an NBA scout, added: "Tim Hardaway does a lot of things very well and

Tim Hardaway

Hardaway's leadership and tenacity on the court in college play were what enabled him to go on to play for the NBA.

makes good decisions. He certainly controls the game."

Brigham Young University guard Michael Smith said, "Tim Hardaway can do it all. Offensively, defensively, and in transition. I would love to play on the same team with a guard like that."

Utah coach Lynn Archibald admired Hardaway, as well. "He's really a strong guard. And he has great acceleration to the basket."

In 1989, UTEP won the WAC postseason tournament behind a league record 67 points in three games by Hardaway, then split a pair of games in the NCAA tournament. The point guard had his best NCAA tourney game in an 85-72 win over LSU as he clicked for 31 points (one shy of his career-high of 32 versus Colorado State that same year).

In a 92-69 second-round loss to Indiana, he was high man for the Miners with 20 points. Following the campaign, Hardaway received loads of honors. He was named to the All-WAC team, was the WAC's Player of the Year, and picked up the MVP award for the WAC's postseason tournament. In addition, Hardaway, then 5'11" tall, was given the Francis Pomeroy Naismith Award recognizing the nation's best collegiate player who is under 6 feet. Plus, he was the MVP in two postseason All-Star games.

Hardaway, the guy who few teams wanted out of high school, finished his career at UTEP as the school's all-time leading scorer with 1,586 points, a record he still holds as of 1998. He also still owns the school standards for career assists, three-point field goals (which began during the 1986-87 season), and steals. His career averages per game were 12.7 points, 4.5 assists, and 2.1 steals. Of the 124 games he appeared in while at UTEP, the Miners won 101. Thirteen times he scored 25 or more points in a game.

"He's a remarkable young man and it was my pleasure to have him here for four years," said Haskins. "It was enjoyable to be around a guy everyday who wanted to be better. I've had three great, great point guards here. First Bobby Joe Hill, who played on my 1966 team, then Nate Archibald and the latest, Tim Hardaway. I'm still looking for another one like Tim."

4
A Draft Day Surprise

The guy who was ignored by college recruits was suddenly getting plenty of attention from pro scouts as his career at the University of Texas at El Paso came to an end. He wasn't considered too small, nor was he thought of as a longshot to make it in the National Basketball Association. The only questions now were, "When will he get drafted and who will draft him?" On June 27, 1989, those questions were answered.

The 1989 draft had a lot of quality players but few who stood out as potential superstars. The bigger names included Pervis Ellison of Louisville, Stacey King of Oklahoma, Danny Ferry of Duke, Sean Elliott of Arizona, Michigan's Glen Rice, and J. R. Reid of North Carolina. Among the guards who were considered first round choices were 6'6" George McCloud of Florida State, Pooh Richardson of UCLA, Nick Anderson of Illi-

Tim Hardaway's tenacious play and reputation as a winning point guard drew the attention of the NBA Warriors and landed him a spot on their team.

Tim Hardaway

The Golden State Warriors surprised many when they chose point guard Tim Hardaway in the 1989 NBA draft. Here coach Don Nelson introduces his new players, Leonard Taylor, left, and Tim Hardaway, right.

nois, Mookie Blaylock from Oklahoma, and Tim Hardaway.

Several teams were looking for a backcourt player, either a playmaking point guard or a shooting guard. The Indiana Pacers, the Dallas Mavericks, the Minnesota Timberwolves, the New Jersey Nets, the Boston Celtics, the Seattle SuperSonics, the Atlanta Hawks, and the Utah Jazz all expressed interest in drafting a guard.

The Sacramento Kings had the first pick in the draft and selected Ellison, and the L.A. Clippers went with Ferry as the second pick. Elliott, Rice, and Reid went next to San Antonio, Miami, and Charlotte. Hardaway, meanwhile, was waiting anxiously to hear his name called.

Chicago grabbed King and then Indiana took the first of the guards, choosing McCloud. Three notches later, Richardson was the second guard picked, by Minnesota. Anderson and Blaylock were picked by the next two teams, Orlando and New Jersey. With the draft's 13th pick, the Celtics called out the name of Mike Smith.

Next up was Golden State, a team that days earlier had signed free agent Sarunas Marciulionis, the first Soviet star to sign an NBA contract. Marciulionis, a 25-year-old, 6'5" guard from Lithuania, was the leading scorer for the Soviet team that captured the gold medal at the 1988 Olympic Games.

As draft day had neared, speculation was that the Warriors, who finished the previous season 43-39 behind Rookie of the Year guard Mitch Richmond and All-Star Chris Mullin, would go for some big inside people. This was a team, buoyed by the acquisition of Marciulionis, that seemed loaded with guards and needy in the middle. The general consensus was that Golden State would go for a power forward. So Hardaway didn't pay much attention as head coach and general manager Don Nelson went up to the podium to announce the Warriors' pick.

But Nelson shocked everyone. He announced that Tim Hardaway of UTEP was Golden State's choice. The move quickly raised questions. One sportswriter asked pointedly, "Why would the Warriors, who had virtually no inside game last season, select Tim Hardaway?" It was a question being asked by many. There was immediate talk of a trade. Nelson lent some credence to that speculation when he indicated that he was still in the market for a power forward.

Prior to the start of the season, the Warriors acquired a handful of players, but no one who would make a real difference. On August 5, meanwhile, Hardaway inked a 4-year deal to play for Golden State.

The 1989-90 season was a wild year for the run-and-gun Warriors. Golden State finished as

Hardaway fights for possession of the ball against Denver Nugget Alex English.

the league's top scoring team, averaging a whopping 116.3 points per game, but more often than not they gave up more points than they scored. They finished the year at 37-45. Hardaway, happy to be within this fast-paced style, played in 79 of the team's 82 games and put up the kind of numbers expected of a first-round choice.

He was picked as the NBA Player of the Week in February. At the end of the season, he averaged 14.7 points and was ninth in the league in assists and 10th in steals. After the campaign was over, Hardaway was one of just two unanimous All-Rookie First Team selections (along with David Robinson). In addition, his teammates showed that they appreciated his enthusiasm by presenting him with the Jack McMahon Award as the most inspirational Warriors player.

Things got better for both Hardaway and the Warriors the next season. Again, Golden State scored in bunches, but this time they were able to put a lid on most of their opponents. The Warriors went 44-38, marking the franchise's best record in nine years. Hardaway averaged 22.9 points per game, ranking him 11th in the league. Teammates Mullin and Richmond, with 25.7 and 23.9 points per game, were ranked 8th and 10th.

At mid-season, Hardaway was chosen to play in his first All-Star Game. Just 24, he became the youngest player at the time to be selected to play in the All-Star Game, where he scored five points and added four assists.

In the playoffs, Golden State shocked San Antonio in the first round, winning the series three games to one. The Los Angeles Lakers ended the Warriors' title hopes in the Western Conference semifinals, four games to one. Hardaway had an excellent playoff series, averaging more than 25 points per game and adding 11.2 assists and 3.1 steals. In the May 14 playoff game against Los Angeles, Hardaway dished out a playoff career–high 20 assists.

The 1990-91 season was a springboard for the 1991-92 season, even though Golden State traded Richmond in November 1991. The Warriors, with the scoring team of Mullin (25.6), Hardaway (23.4), and Marciulionis (18.9), reeled off 118.7 points per game and amassed a 55-27 record.

But the playoffs proved to be a disappointment for Hardaway and his teammates as the Seattle SuperSonics bounced the Warriors out of contention in the very first round, three games to one, despite an average of 24.5 points and 7.3 assists a game by Hardaway. For the second straight year, Hardaway posted an NBA playoff record eight steals in a game. During the postseason, Golden State got some satisfaction when Nelson earned his third Coach of the Year award and All-NBA Team honors went to Mullin (first team) and Hardaway (second team).

As fine a year as it was for Hardaway, there was one night in particular that he would like to forget. On December 27, 1991, Hardaway missed all 17 of his field goal attempts in a game against San Antonio, setting an NBA record in futility. On a better note, his 10 assists per game ranked him third in the league. Hardaway also made the most of his second All-Star Game appearance that year, scoring 14 points and dishing out seven assists in 20 minutes.

As good as the 1991-92 season was, the 1992-93 season was the complete opposite for the Warriors. Injury-riddled from the start, Golden State stumbled to a 34-48 record. Fourteen players were sidelined for a total of 312 games. No one escaped the rash of injuries. Marciulionis and first-round draft pick Latrell Sprewell went down in November, followed by Keith Jennings, Jeff Grayer, Bill Owens, and Chris Mullin.

In March, Hardaway joined the list with a badly bruised right knee. Despite playing in only 66 games, Hardaway finished as Golden State's second-leading scorer with 21.5 points a game, while adding 10.6 assists to make him only the fifth NBA player to score more than 20 points and record 10 assists in consecutive seasons. Hardaway's mid-season numbers were good enough to get him into the All-Star Game again. This time, he fired in 26 points and added six assists in 21 minutes.

As rough as they had it that season, however, the Warriors were not that far away from having a winning season. They lost 10 games by three points or less.

The 1993-94 season was a dream come true for Golden State, but a nightmare for Hardaway. While his team rolled to a 50-32 mark behind Sprewell and newly acquired first-round pick Chris Webber, Hardaway's season ended before it began. In a preseason game against Orlando, he blew out his left knee.

A Draft Day Surprise

Hardaway's enthusiasm earned him the Jack McMahon Award as the most inspirational Warrior player in 1990.

At first, Hardaway thought he might be able to play later in the season, but reality soon set in. On November 2, he was officially placed on the injured list. His season was over, and in December he underwent successful reconstructive surgery. It was a frustrating year for Hardaway, who had to watch from the sidelines as his teammates enjoyed a terrific season.

For Golden State, the success came with an element of surprise. Not only did Hardaway miss the entire season due to injury, but so did Sarunas Marciulionis. In addition, Chris Mullin missed the team's first 20 games. Yet behind Sprewell's team-leading 21 points per game and Webber's 17.5, the Warriors prevailed to post the franchise's fourth 50-win season. But the team's season ended abruptly in the first round of the playoffs when it was eliminated by the Phoenix Suns in three straight games.

Unfortunately for Hardaway, his injury cost him an appearance with Dream Team II, an NBA All-Star squad that went on to win the 1994 USA Basketball World Championships.

Golden State's 1994-95 season was a disaster. Even with Hardaway returning to chip in with 20 points and 9.3 assists per game (third best in the league), the Warriors crashed to a 26-56 record. Nelson stepped down as coach and general manager in February and Bob Lanier took over as the interim head coach. Nothing helped, though, as Golden State sank deeper and deeper in the standings. Hardaway was injured again, and this time it was his left wrist. On March 19, he was lost for the season.

It didn't get much better for Golden State the following year. And for Hardaway, it got worse. Under new head coach Rick Adelman, Hardaway lost his starting job to B. J. Armstrong, and it was clear he was unhappy about it. Adelman's decision to pull Hardaway from the starting lineup, together with some other choices he made as coach, divided the team.

"They benched Tim, benched Chris Mullin for Jerome Kersey, and benched me for Clifford Rozi-

A Draft Day Surprise

On his way to the basket, Tim Hardaway dribbles his way past Houston Rocket Eric Floyd.

er," recalled Hardaway's former teammate, Rony Seikaly. "Those were bad years for everybody all around, from the organization down to the players. There was a lot of talent on that team, a lot of good players, but injuries kept everybody apart."

"I don't think either one of us made the decision," said Armstrong, who had come to Gold-

Tim Hardaway plays against the New Jersey Nets' Yinka Dare in a pre-season game before the disastrous 1995-96 season under new coach Rick Adelman.

en State from Chicago. "The decision was made by the coach."

"He was coming off the injury, trying to find himself, get himself back going," said former teammate Chris Gatling. "Tim wasn't playing up to par, and they moved B. J. to starting point guard and Tim became the sixth man. That really caused a lot of animosity with him because he had been a starter his whole time there, and now he's got to come off the bench in a back-up role. That didn't look good in his eyes.

"The team thought [Tim] should be starting, but that wasn't our call. It was the coach's call. It went downhill from there. He wasn't starting and there was one game he didn't even get into. He was really frustrated and disappointed in the organization."

The situation finally came to a head on February 22, 1996, when Hardaway and Gatling were traded to Pat Riley's Miami Heat for Kevin Willis and Bimbo Coles. To this day, Hardaway still harbors bad feelings toward Adelman because he believes the coach did not treat him right. Hardaway and Gatling were satisfied at the end of the season when the Heat made the playoffs and the Warriors, who finished at 36-46, did not.

Hardaway played for Golden State for a little more than five seasons, not including the full year he missed due to his injured knee. During that short career, he became one of the team's top-ranked players. He was third in steals (821), 10th in scoring average (19.8), second in assists (3,926), first in three-point field goal attempts (1,607), and first in three-point field goals made (602). He is also ranked among the team's top season record-holders in several categories.

He may have accumulated a host of records at Golden State, but when the trade to Miami came, Hardaway's thoughts were on the future, not the past. He was determined to prove to everyone that his career was far from over.

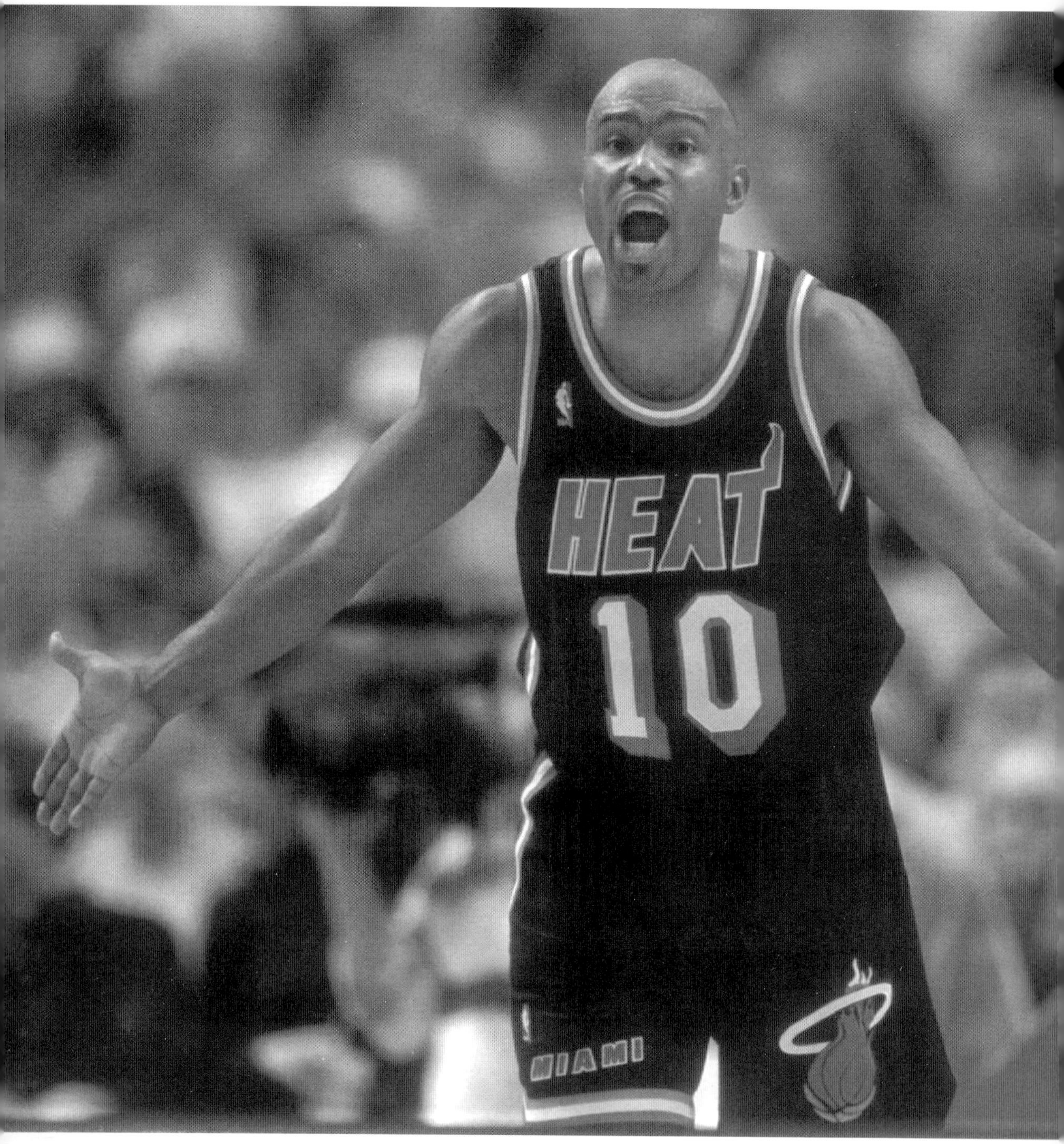
HEAT
10
MIAMI

5
A New Beginning in Miami

Some people wondered if Tim Hardaway's career was fizzling out. Injuries had cost him parts of the previous three seasons, and with Warrior coach Rick Adelman showing little confidence in Hardaway, they just weren't sure what Hardaway could do at this point in his career. Through it all, Hardaway kept his cool, knowing that he would get another chance to prove his worth. His opportunity came in Miami.

The same day Hardaway and Gatling were traded to the Heat, Miami's president and head coach, Pat Riley, made two other deals, taking Walt Williams and Tyrone Corbin from Sacramento and Tony Smith from Phoenix.

Miami had entered the NBA for the 1988-89 season as an expansion team. Riley, who had previously coached the Los Angeles Lakers and the New York Knicks, was determined to make the young Heat organization a perennial contender sooner, rather than later.

Tim Hardaway was traded to the Miami Heat in February of 1996.

Tim Hardaway

Philadelphia 76er Ed Pinckney tries to guard the Miami Heat's Hardaway in his first game on the Miami team.

On paper, the Hardaway acquisition seemed to be at odds with Riley's coaching philosophy. Hardaway was coming from a run-and-gun style at Golden State that featured a quick-paced attack and the opportunity to throw up a lot of three-pointers. In Miami, the offense was more deliberate and defense played a much bigger role. It was similar to the style Hardaway played at UTEP.

"A lot of people thought, 'Oh boy, Tim's going to play for Pat Riley—wrong place for him,'" said Hardaway's former assistant coach at UTEP, Russ Bradburd. "But Tim had already been through that transition."

The trade for Hardaway earned quick dividends. In his first start for the Heat on February 25, 1996, Hardaway rang up a team-leading 20 points and nine assists, helping Miami to push past Philadelphia, 108-101. Down by 10 early in the third quarter, it was Hardaway who keyed a 25-9 surge to give the Heat the lead for good.

The Heat, struggling to make the playoffs prior to the trade, over the next few weeks were suddenly in the postseason picture. And, on April 19, the franchise, propelled by center Alonzo Mourning and Hardaway, tied the team mark for wins in a season at 42 with a 106-100 victory over Milwaukee. While Mourning dropped in 28 points, Hardaway scored 17 points and set a team record for assists with 19. That same night, Golden State got ousted from playoff contention with a loss to the Portland Trail Blazers.

The Heat lost its season finale, yet finished the year at 42-40, its best record since the 1993-94 season. The team was glad to be in the playoffs, but unhappy to see that their first round match-up was with the Chicago Bulls, who unceremoniously dumped Miami in three straight. Hardaway averaged 17.7 points and more than five assists during the three-game series.

Hardaway finished the season with some pretty impressive numbers, especially since he didn't play all that much with Golden State. He averaged a combined 15.2 points and eight assists a game, but his stats didn't surprise everyone.

"I think Golden State just got disenchanted [with Hardaway], which they seem to have done with a lot of players," said Atlanta Hawks coach Lenny Wilkens. "You've got to give a guy a chance to heal. Tim has great talent. They just gave up on him, that's all."

"Hardaway has always been a real aggressive and good ballplayer," noted Charlotte's Vernon Maxwell. "I knew once he got his knee back and rhythm back that he'd do well."

"When we got to Miami, he was a totally different player," said Gatling. "I couldn't believe it . . . He was really amazing. There were a lot of things I had never seen him do before. A lot of it was because he wasn't in as good a shape

Tim Hardaway tries to use strong defense against the legendary Michael Jordan in the 1996 NBA Eastern Conference playoffs. The Bulls won the series in three straight games.

[because of the injuries], a lot of it was because of Riley's training."

Many of his new teammates appreciated what Hardaway brought to the team.

"He's a great player," said Dan Majerle. "He makes everyone else around him a great player. He can take it to the hole or score from outside. He can post up which makes him even more dangerous. He does everything a good point guard is supposed to do. He finds open men or he can create for himself or create for other people. There is no weakness in his game. He's just a fantastic point guard."

"He makes everybody else better," added Mourning. "He feeds the ball in the right spots. He has great court awareness. He does an extremely great job of distributing the ball and getting it into the paint. He kind of makes me run the court. I know that if I run hard, I'm going to get the basketball. He gives me easy baskets in transition."

"I know when I played with him he always found me for baskets," said former Golden State teammate Rony Seikaly. "Tim is a great player because he makes people around him better. He creates easy shots for them, whether open layups or dunks."

Gatling had known for a long time what Hardaway was capable of.

"He tries to bring everybody up, whether you're playing good or bad," said Gatling, who left Miami for Dallas after the season as a free agent. "He would always tell me to work hard, you'll get your chance. Just be ready. And then when I got my chance I was ready. So I owe a lot to him."

Yet as well as Hardaway played for Miami, there was no guarantee he would return for the

1996-97 season. There were a few good free agent point guards available that off-season. Hardaway was a free agent himself and although he was anxious to return to Miami, he was being courted by Houston.

Riley initially wanted to keep his options open and considered signing one of a trio of younger point guards—Gary Payton, Chris Childs, or Robert Pack. Finally, he decided Hardaway was the right choice, and he signed him to a four-year deal.

Buoyed by his new contract, Hardaway led Miami to its first-ever divisional title in 1997, beating out the highly touted Knicks for the Atlantic Division crown. The Heat clinched the title on April 10 with a 93-83 win over the Detroit Pistons. Hardaway was high man with 30 points. As a team, the Heat finished with a franchise best record of 61-21. For Hardaway, it was just the kind of season he had hoped for. He knocked in 20.3 points, dished out 8.6 assists, and made nearly two steals a game.

It was a season of highlight film material for Hardaway, but few snippets matched his performance on March 7 when he drilled in a career-high 45 points in an overtime win over Washington. At mid-season Hardaway was picked to play in the All-Star Game for the first time since 1993; it was his fourth All-Star appearance. He responded with a 10-point game.

Hardaway played well in the playoffs, leading the Heat past Orlando and New York before losing to Michael Jordan and the Chicago Bulls in five games in the Eastern Conference finals. In the fifth and deciding game with Chicago, the Heat followed a format it set during the previous four games that made the outcome pretty

The Miami Heat lost in the fifth game of the 1997 Eastern Conference play-offs to the Chicago Bulls. Despite the loss, the 1996-97 season saw Hardaway at the top of his form—one of the best point guards in the NBA.

predictable. Miami simply lost its scoring touch. Hardaway, who played all 81 games during the regular season, played all 17 playoff games as well. He cranked out 18.7 points and seven assists per game.

By the end of the season, it was clear that Hardaway, who wears the number 10 on his jersey and the initials M.E.E. on the back of his size 13 sneakers for his late grandmother, Minny E. Eubanks, had proven the doubters wrong. In fact, his game had risen to another level, and he was playing better than he ever had with Golden State. He was now uniformly considered one of the premier point guards in the league. Few point guards could match him when it came to forcing the tempo of a game, shooting from deep, or making things happen off a dribble.

The 1997 *Street & Smith's Pro Basketball* preview magazine for the 1997-98 season said: "Hardaway, rejuvenated by Riley's system, is coming off his finest season. He doesn't have the blinding quickness he once had, but he has as much court savvy as anyone in the game today."

"He's better now then when he was with Golden State," said Gatling. "At Golden State he had a pretty good supporting cast around him, but he didn't have a big man that he could throw to. Now he has a legitimate big man in Mourning."

"He was quicker when he was with Golden State," said Seikaly. "Now he's playing a different kind of basketball. He's team-oriented. He's playing great defense. He's playing phenomenal."

"He's worked himself back into great shape," added Childs, who now plays for the Knicks. "He's got his knee back to where he's even deadlier because he plays smarter than when he did when he was a younger guy and had the legs. I don't think people give him much credit as being an intelligent ballplayer, which he is. He has shown he knows a lot and can handle any situation."

While the Heat, riddled with injuries, did not play as well as in the 1997-98 season, they repeated as Atlantic Division champs—and by a good margin. Hardaway was injury-free and was Miami's model of consistency. He capped the regular season with averages of 19.6 points, 9.1 assists, and 2.1 steals per game. Perhaps more impressive is that he played in every Heat game, regular season and playoffs, for the second straight season. Again he was selected to play in the All-Star Game.

"He has a lot of confidence in his game," said teammate Eric Murdock. "A lot of times that confidence trickles down through the team. When we are playing well it's usually started by Tim. He gets everybody involved, gets them hustling and playing offense. He's a point guard who doesn't have any weaknesses. He has a total all-around game. He averages close to 20 points and nine assists a game. Not too many people can say that. When you can score that many points and still get your teammates involved that's a special kind of player."

"Tim is more or less the heart of this team," acknowledged Terry Mills. "He provides energy and focus for this team. As Tim goes, so goes the Heat."

Miami's chief competition in the Atlantic that season was the surprising New Jersey Nets, and of course, the New York Knicks. The Knick rivalry continues, and whenever the two teams get together, it's a battle to the finish.

"We always bring out the best in them," said Hardaway, who prefers to downplay the rivalry.

Hardaway shoots over the heads of New York Knicks Charlie Ward and Larry Johnson in the 1998 NBA playoffs as the Heat/Knicks rivalry continued.

"I have respect for the Knicks because they come out and play hard and don't lay down. I've never seen them roll over. They dive for the ball, try for loose balls. They give you a run for your money every night out, which makes them very dangerous. I just want it to be a regular old game [when we play them] but the media wants to make it a rivalry and hype it all up."

"We seem to bring out the best in that team," agreed Hardaway's teammate, P. J. Brown. "Every game we play against the Knicks is a playoff game and we have to realize that. When they play the Miami Heat, that's their season and we should feel the same way."

"This rivalry has got a history," said New York Knicks coach Jeff Van Gundy. "It's hotly contested. Very hotly contested games. Maybe you don't have high scoring games, but if you like competitive, intense basketball, then that's what you get with these two teams."

It certainly was the case during the regular season when the teams split the four-game series with all four games being decided by six points or less. The first round of the playoffs were also very closely contested, and the two teams squared off for a best-of-five series.

The series appeared to be in Miami's favor since the Knicks were playing without their All-Star center Patrick Ewing, who missed most of the season with an injury. That feeling was strengthened after Game 1, a 94-79 blowout by the Heat. But New York wasn't to be taken lightly, and it bounced back to take the second game, 96-86. The Heat won Game 3, 91-85.

The next playoff game between the two teams ended in turmoil. As the final seconds ticked away in New York's 90-85 Game 4 win, a fracas

A New Beginning in Miami

Tim Hardaway drives past New York Knick Charlie Ward in the 1998 NBA playoffs.

broke out on court. When the dust cleared this time, Mourning was lost for Game 5, as were New York's Larry Johnson and Chris Mills. All three were suspended for their involvement in the scuffle.

The loss of Mourning was too much for Miami to overcome, and the Knicks crushed the Heat, 98-81. The Heat's promising season ended on a down note. For Miami to win the clincher, Hardaway would have had to have a major game. Even though he scored a team-high 21 points, it wasn't enough to carry the team.

"We just didn't come out with the need or the energy to win," the dejected Hardaway said afterwards. "I knew I had to do a lot in order for us to win. I just didn't do a lot. I should've put up 30 shots early." The way his team played, however, not even that would have helped. It was one of those games that Hardaway only wanted to forget. The sooner the better.

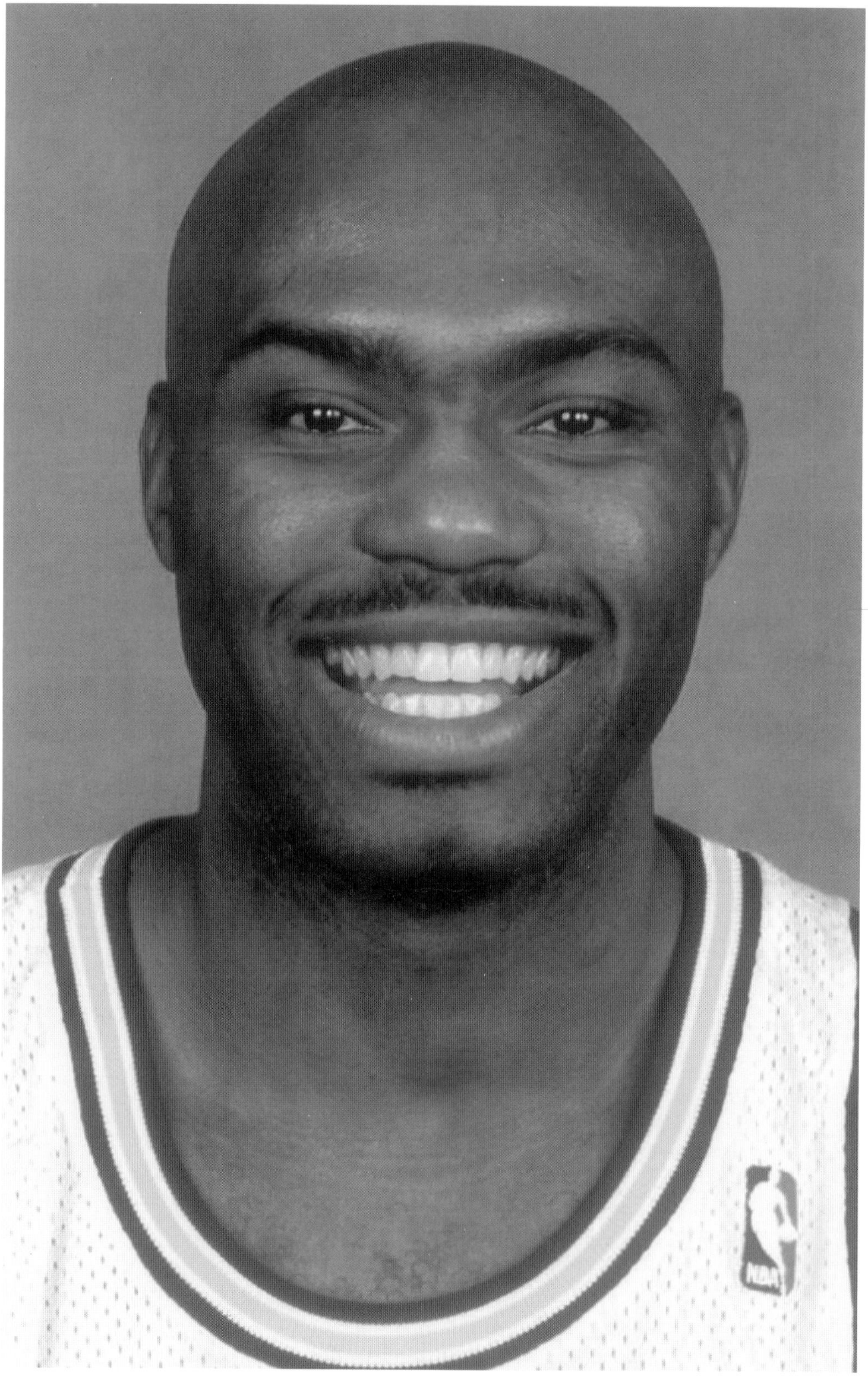

6

THE ELUSIVE RING

Tim Hardaway is thrilled to have made it to the NBA, to have played in All-Star and playoff games, and to have played on division championship teams. One thing is missing, however.

A championship ring. That remains his one and only pro basketball goal.

"Win a championship," he said. "That's it. I don't need any other goals. To play on a championship team, that's my only goal."

Whether he ever plays on a championship team or not, many already consider Hardaway a champion. And he's not just a winner to his mother and father or his wife, Yolanda, and his two children, Tim Jr. and Nia. In the Miami Heat's magazine, one of the most popular features is a children's Q & A with Hardaway. Fans in Miami and elsewhere, including those who are less fortunate, appreciate Hardaway. He is still very active in cancer causes, donating $20 for every

Tim Hardaway's enthusiasm and love of basketball made him the heart of his team.

"He's a basketball player in and out," said one NBA coach. And Tim Hardaway would prove it time and again.

assist he makes to the American Cancer Society and the Cancer Caring Center.

On the court, Hardaway's opponents have the utmost respect for him, too. Anyone who has ever defended against Hardaway knows they have their work cut out for them. "He's one of the toughest guards to play against because he has so much range," said Derek Harper. "You just have to stay in front of him, which is easier said than done. If his jump shot is on, you're in for a long night. If he's hitting that three and that jumper consistently, then it's a tough one."

"He's like a little general," said Kobe Bryant. "I try to use my length when I go up against him. Try and make him shoot over me. But you gotta hope he's having an off night or something like that."

"You can't give him open shots," Atlanta Hawks coach Lenny Wilkens said. "You've got to play him [tight]. You've got to match up quickly because in transition he'll get the quick shots. You've got to make him work. You can't let him dictate the game."

"He's a basketball player in and out," said Charlotte coach Dave Cowens. "He's street-smart

The Elusive Ring

and tough as nails. He has the ability to take a game over."

New Jersey Nets coach John Calipari said, "When the game's on the line, Timmy shoots." More often than not, the shots go in.

Hardaway, meanwhile, is modest about his game. "I am very confident, aggressive," he said. "I'm an alright defensive player, a good offensive player—and I'm very competitive. I just come out to play every night. I try and be steady. Sometimes you'll have it, sometimes you won't. You just have to be steady."

As far as his grade school coach is concerned, Hardaway's success is easily attributable.

"The thing that makes certain people successful is because of their ability to listen to their elders, their advisors," says Donald Pittman. "The thing that's remarkable about Tim, his strength, is that he has always listened to whoever the person is in charge. He gives his undivided attention, to the point where it's really exceptional."

And that's the kind of advice that Hardaway likes to offer to aspiring basketball players.

"I tell them to work hard and not let anybody

Hardaway's advice to young players is: work hard and don't let anyone shake your confidence.

take their confidence away," he says. "Work on all aspects of your game. Defense, shooting, layups, all that stuff. And stay in school because you never know when all this stuff is going to end."

In his case, Tim Hardaway is hoping that it doesn't end before he's wearing a new ring.

CHRONOLOGY

1966   Born September 1 in Chicago, Illinois.

1989   Completes four-year career at the University of Texas at El Paso (UTEP) as school's all-time leading scorer with 1,586 points and is honored as Western Athletic Conference Player of the Year in his senior year, when he averaged 22 points and 5.4 assists per game. Receives the 1989 Frances Pomeroy Naismith Hall of Fame Award as the nation's best college player under six feet; drafted in the first round (14th overall) by the Golden State Warriors

1990   Is a unanimous selection to the 1989-90 NBA All-Rookie First Team

1991   Selected to play in his first of five All-Star Games

1991-92   Finishes season with a career-high scoring average of 23.4

1993-94   Misses season due to injury

1994   Dishes out a career-high 22 assists versus the Orlando Magic on December 16; comes back from missed season with 20.1 points and 9.3 assists per game

1996   Traded to the Miami Heat on February 22

1997   Scores a career-high 45 points against the Washington Wizards on March 7

1997   Scores a playoff career–high 38 points against the New York Knicks on May 8; named to the 1996-97 All-NBA First Team

STATISTICS

TIM HARDAWAY
NBA REGULAR SEASON

Season	Team	G	FG%	3P%	FT%	STL	BLK	RPG	APG	PPG
1989-90	Golden State	79	.471	.274	.764	165	12	3.9	8.7	14.7
1990-91	Golden State	82	.476	.385	.803	214	12	4.0	9.7	22.9
1991-92	Golden State	81	.461	.338	.766	164	13	3.8	10.0	23.4
1992-93	Golden State	66	.447	.330	.744	116	12	4.0	10.6	21.5
1993-94	Golden State	Injured - Did Not Play								
1994-95	Golden State	62	.427	.378	.760	88	12	3.1	9.3	20.1
1995-96	GS-Miami	80	.422	.364	.790	132	17	2.9	8.0	15.2
1996-97	Miami	81	.415	.344	.799	151	9	3.4	8.6	20.3
1997-98	Miami	81	.431	.351	.781	136	16	3.7	8.3	18.9
Totals		612	.445	.352	.777	1166	103	3.6	9.1	19.6
Playoffs		33	.412	.330	.759	77	8	3.7	8.1	21.1

G	games played
FG%	field goal percentage
3P%	three-point percentage
FT%	free-throw percentage
STL	steals
BLK	blocks
RPG	rebounds per game
APG	assists per game
PPG	points per game

FURTHER READING

Price, S.L. "Hot Hand." *Sports Illustrated*, May 5, 1997.

Relin, David Oliver. "Buggin' Out." *React Newspaper Supplement*, May 11-17, 1998.

"Repeating as Atlantic Division champs would be extraordinary, since every team is improved." *Street & Smith's Pro Basketball*, September 1997.

Vancil, Mark. *NBA Basketball Basics.* New York: Sterling Publishing Company, Inc., 1995.

Wilker, Josh. *The Head Coaches.* Philadephia: Chelsea House Publishers, 1998.

ABOUT THE AUTHOR

Dan Hirshberg is the President of CHP Communications, Hackettstown, N.J., and covers pro basketball and boxing for *The Trentonian*, Trenton, N.J. He is the author of *Phil Rizzuto: A Yankee Tradition*, as well as books on Emmitt Smith, John Elway, and Lawrence Taylor for Chelsea House's Football Legends Series. He lives in Hackettstown with his wife, Susan, and two children, Nathan and Melanie.

INDEX

Adelman, Rick, 42-43, 45, 47
All-Rookie First Team, 38
All-WAC team, 31, 32
Anderson, Nick, 22, 35, 36
Archibald, Lynn, 32
Armstrong, B. J., 43-44
Austin, Isaac, 13
Boston Celtics, 36
Bradburd, Russ, 25-26, 27-28, 48
Brigham Young University, 32
Brown, P. J., 13-14, 54
Bryant, Kobe, 58
Calipari, John, 59
Carver High School, 20-21
Charlotte Hornets, 11
Chicago Bulls, 10, 48, 51
Coles, Bimbo, 45
Colorado State University, 33
Corbin, Tyrone, 47
Cowens, Dave, 58-59
Cummings, Terry, 20
Detroit Pistons, 51
Eubanks, Minny E., 52
Ewing, Patrick, 11, 12, 14, 54
Feitl, Dave, 27
Finn, Dan, 21
Floyd, Tim, 26
Francis Pomeroy Naismith Award, 33
Gatling, Chris, 44, 45, 47, 49, 50, 52
Golden State Warriors, 36, 37-44, 47-48, 49, 52
Grayer, Jeff, 40
Griffith, Yolanda, 20
Hardaway, Anfernee, 10
Hardaway, Donald, 15, 17-18
Hardaway, Gwendolyn, 15
Hardaway, Nia, 57
Hardaway, Timothy
  in All-Star Games, 39, 40, 41, 51, 53

childhood, 17-20
college years, 26-33
with Golden State Warriors, 37-45
in high school, 20-23
honors, 31, 33, 38, 39
injuries, 40-42
with Miami Heat, 47-55
in 1989 NBA draft, 35-37
in playoff games, 9-15, 39, 51
statistics, 30-31, 33, 39, 41, 45, 48, 51, 53
Hardaway, Timothy Jr., 15, 57
Hardaway, Yolanda, 57
Haskins, Don, 25, 27, 29-30, 33
Houston, Allan, 14
Indiana University, 31, 32
Jack McMahon Award, 38
Jackson, Jeep, 27, 29
Jennings, Keith, 40
Johnson, Larry, 14, 55
Kersey, Jerome, 43
Kohn Elementary School, 18
Lanier, Bob, 42
Los Angeles Lakers, 39, 47
Louisiana State University, 33
Majerle, Dan, 10, 50
Marciulionis, Sarunas, 36-37, 40, 42
Maxwell, Vernon, 49
Miami Heat, 9-15, 47, 51-52, 53-54
Mills, Chris, 55
Mills, Terry, 53
Mourning, Alonzo, 9, 13, 15, 48, 50, 52, 55
Mullin, Chris, 37, 38, 39, 40, 42
Murdock, Eric, 53
Musselman, Bill, 31
Nelson, Don, 37, 39, 42
New Jersey Nets, 53

New York Knicks, 9-15, 47, 51, 53-54
Oakley, Charles, 13
Orlando Magic, 10, 15, 41, 51
Owens, Bill, 40
Phoenix Suns, 42
Pittman, Donald, 18-19, 20, 21, 22, 59
Portland Trail Blazers, 48
Richmond, Mike, 29
Richmond, Mitch, 37, 38, 39, 40
Riley, Pat, 10, 12, 13, 45, 47, 48, 49, 51, 52
Robinson, David, 38
Rozier, Clifford, 42-43
Russell, Cazzie, 20
Sacramento Kings, 36
Sandle, Chris, 29
Seattle SuperSonics, 40
Seikaly, Rony, 42-43, 50, 52
Smith, Juden, 27
Smith, Michael, 32, 36
Smith, Tony, 47
Sprewell, Latrell, 40, 42
Starks, John, 14
Thomas, Isiah, 21-22
University of Texas at El Paso (UTEP) (Miners), 23, 25, 26-33, 35, 48
Van Gundy, Jeff, 54
Vitale, Dick, 31
Wallace, John, 13
Walters, Bob, 20, 22-23
Ward, Charlie, 11, 13-14
Webber, Chris, 40
Western Athletic Conference (WAC), 27, 29, 31, 32
Western Illinois University, 25
Wilkens, Lenny, 49, 58
Williams, Buck, 14
Willis, Kevin, 45

PHOTO CREDITS
AP WORLD/WIDE PHOTOS: pp. 2, 8, 10, 11, 14, 16, 18, 22, 28, 32, 34, 36, 38, 41, 43, 44, 46, 48, 49, 52, 54, 55, 56, 58, 59; EL PASO TIMES, pp. 24, 31